WADDLE

A book of fun for penguin lovers

Compiled by Lloyd Spencer Davis

EXISLE
PUBLISHING

Introduction

Penguins. We love them. They are instantly recognizable. Seemingly upright caricatures of us, it is easy to bond with these black and white 'little people'. They have become perennial favourites of cartoonists, and that's the thing about penguins: they are fun. Comical. They put a smile on our faces.

Of course, real penguins are a lot more than just funny. They are tough. Penguins are the world's only '100-degree birds', breeding in environments from –60°C to +40°C (–76°F to 104°F). They can dive to great depths — over 600 metres (328 fathoms) in the case of the Emperor penguin — and exist for long periods in water so cold that it would kill us within minutes. They have all the grace and agility of ballet dancers in water, but it is the way they comport themselves on land that

so endears them to us: they waddle.

From *March of the Penguins* to *Happy Feet*, penguins have been box-office hits that appeal to the whole family. We admire their steely determination and rejoice in their amusing antics. We are fascinated with their love lives. The persona of penguins is, in many respects, how we'd like to see ourselves — as fun-loving and with a better sense of morals and dress.

This compilation of quotations about penguins reflects that focus on fun. You can dip into and out of it at your leisure, but you can also read the book from cover to cover for some added pleasure. The intention is to put a grin on your face and a warm feeling in your heart — all thanks to these delightful creatures that don't just walk, but waddle.

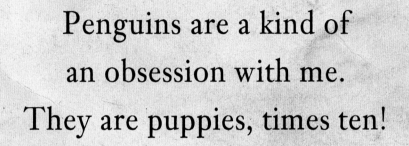

Penguins are a kind of
an obsession with me.
They are puppies, times ten!

JIM CARREY

The penguin loves you too.

ED SHEERAN

Penguins mate for life. That doesn't surprise me much, because they all look alike. It's not like they are going to meet a better-looking penguin someday.

ELLEN DEGENERES

What's the two things they tell you
are healthiest to eat? Chicken and
fish. You know what you should do?
Combine them, eat a penguin.

DAVE ATTELL

Falling fast and hard like a
penguin who hasn't bought the
whole flightless scenario.

JENNIFER RARDIN

The Gentoo is the most strongly marked of all the smaller varieties of penguins as far as colouring is concerned, and it far surpasses the Adelie in weight of legs and breast, the points that particularly appealed to us.

ERNEST SHACKLETON

If ever the difficulties of your
life seem overwhelming,
consider the prospect of being
eaten alive by savage penguins
and rejoice that such horrors
are unknown to you.

A.L. KENNEDY

There were penguins, so agile in the water that they have been taken for the rapid bonitos, heavy and awkward as they are on the ground; they were uttering harsh cries, a large assembly, sober in gesture, but extravagant in clamor.

JULES VERNE

I have often had the impression that, to penguins, man is just another penguin — different, less predictable, occasionally violent, but tolerable company when he sits still and minds his own business.

BERNARD STONEHOUSE

All the birds had flown away,
save only the great,
grotesque penguins.

H.P. LOVECRAFT

Penguins don't waste their time trying to fly. They're unique. They know they were built for the water.

SYDNEY KNIGHT

Again and again we are confronted with the reality — some might say the problem — of sharing our space with other living things, be they dogs, trees, fish or penguins.

JONATHAN SAFRAN FOER

You can never have too
many penguins.

ROBYN MUNDY

It is a received opinion that
penguins never go far from land,
and that the sight of them is a sure
indication of its vicinity.

JAMES COOK

One dark night we were surrounded by numerous seals and penguins, which made such strange noises, that the officer on watch reported he could hear the cattle bellowing on shore.

CHARLES DARWIN

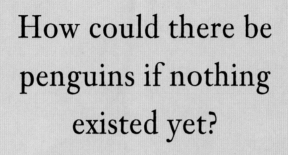

How could there be penguins if nothing existed yet?

DAVID S. ATKINSON

Antarctica. You know, that
giant continent at the bottom
of the Earth that's ruled by
penguins and seals.

C.B. COOK

The Adelie penguin on land or ice is almost wholly ludicrous ... but the Adelie penguin in the water is another thing; as it darts to and fro a fathom or two below the surface, as it leaps porpoise-like into the air or swims skimmingly over the rippling surface of a pool, it excites nothing but admiration.

ROBERT FALCON SCOTT

'No, I mean it.
You don't look good.'
This from a guy who has all the
sex appeal of a penguin.

CASSANDRA CLARE

He hadn't just found a sign of water on a destitute planet, he'd found a sign that the same planet had penguins. Those would be two fundamentally different breakthroughs.

MANDY ASHCRAFT

These birds walk erect, with a stately carriage. They carry their heads high, with their wings drooping like two arms, and, as their tails project from their body in a line with the legs, the resemblance to a human figure is very striking, and would be apt to deceive the spectator at a casual glance or in the gloom of the evening.

EDGAR ALLAN POE

You're turning into a
penguin. Stop it.

DOUGLAS ADAMS

The biblical account of Noah's Ark and the Flood is perhaps the most implausible story for fundamentalists to defend. Where, for example, while loading his ark, did Noah find penguins and polar bears in Palestine?

JUDITH HAYES

I have taken the liberty of quoting at length … from the gospels of the Emperor penguins. To them I owe a special debt of gratitude for their remarkable patience.

DONALD FINKEL

I felt as lonely and desolate as
a man suddenly fallen from the
clouds into an unknown town on
the Antarctic Continent built of
ice and inhabited by Penguins.

W.N.P. BARBELLION

Penguins are the really ideal
example of monogamy.

RICH LOWRY

They say penguins mate
for life … And I want to
be your penguin.

BELLE AURORA

And so you ask yourself:
'If a penguin can have a
worthwhile, stimulating
relationship, why the hell
can't I?'

BRADLEY TREVOR GREIVE

I walk like a duck: very
straight up and down.
Or like a penguin.
It's a dead giveaway
that I'm a dancer.

DAVID HALLBERG

Gentoo penguins mate for life. Whereas Adelie penguins prostitute themselves for rocks. I'd like to be your Gentoo penguin.

PENNY REID

Our wings serve as flippers
that carry us across the ocean;
not in the sky!
Why, us penguins have so
much fun time in the water,
we don't even want to fly!

JASMINE JEAN

I've never been in love, but if a penguin can find a soul mate, I'm sure I can, too.

REBEKAH CRANE

I already own a penguin.

WOODY ALLEN

Everyone has their weaknesses.
Some people smoke. I collect
stuffed penguins. If you won't
tell, I won't.

LAURELL K. HAMILTON

He moves with the predatory
grace of a penguin.

SARAH REES BRENNAN

There's a tendency to
think tap's had its day,
but *Happy Feet* kept us in
the race. That penguin
is our Shirley Temple.

SAVION GLOVER

Not only in their upright walk, but also in their manners and antics, these birds remind one strikingly of human beings. It has been remarked that an Emperor is the very image of 'an old gentleman in evening dress', and the resemblance is indeed very noticeable.

ROALD AMUNDSEN

I love penguins.

QUVENZHANÉ WALLIS

I think penguins are cute.

ZOOEY DESCHANEL

Because I am the most
shallow person in the
world, my mission is to
see men's formal wear
change a little bit. It is
too rigid! Everybody
looks like a penguin!

STEVEN COJOCARU

Once a penguin finds its perfect other penguin, they stay together pretty much forever.

ANNA STANISZEWSKI

Have you ever noticed that people look like either rodents or birds? And you can classify them that way, like, I definitely have more of a rodent face, but you look like a penguin.

JESSE ANDREWS

In the evening every man
looks the same. Like
penguins. Women have a
special dress for that event;
men, the same tuxedo.

ROBERTO CAVALLI

He looks about as happy as a
penguin in a microwave.

SID WADDELL

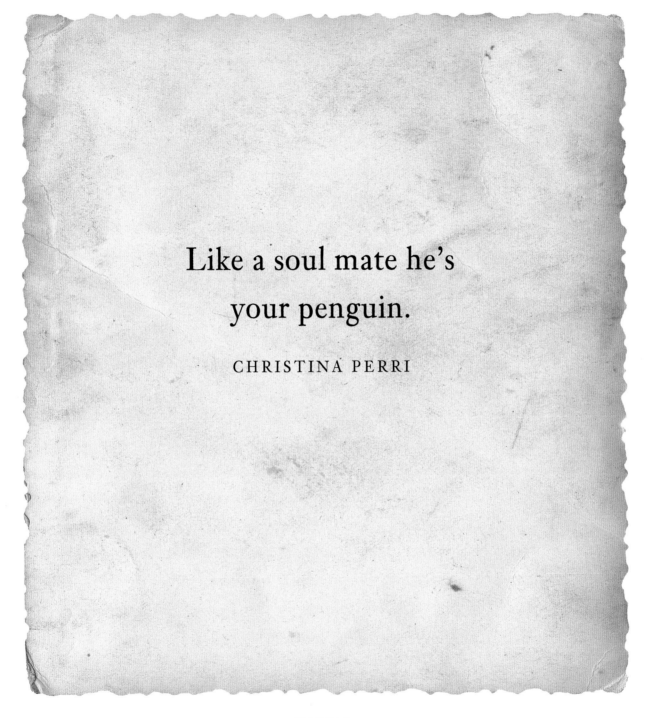

Like a soul mate he's
your penguin.

CHRISTINA PERRI

WADDLE

I know what nuns are, kind of.
It's just I never saw one. I didn't know
they looked like penguins.

LESLEY HOWARTH

She said seals sexually assault penguins and deserved to be clubbed. That woman is nuttier than a Snickers bar.

L.H. COSWAY

She smiled with the warmth
of a penguin.

KIM HARRISON

There have been better attempts at marching, and they have been made by penguins.

TERRY PRATCHETT

My friends just call me the hideous penguin boy.

TIM BURTON

Our babies are like penguins; penguin babies can't exist unless more than one person is taking care of them. They just can't keep going.

ALISON GOPNIK

I suggest we depict penguins as callous and unfeeling creatures who insist on bringing up their children in what is little more than a large chest freezer.

JASPER FFORDE

There I was a month later,
standing still with an egg under
my belly, remembering ...
I was the one who had brought
up the subject.

ALESSANDRO BOFFA

Verily, her ways were as the ways
of the inscrutable penguins in
building their inscrutable nests,
which baffle all science, and
make a fool of a sage.

HERMAN MELVILLE

I want to be your personal penguin.

SANDRA BOYNTON

Colder than a bucket of
penguin shit!

THOMAS PYNCHON

Not all babies learn to play chess
or hunt penguins, or play
the didgeridoo …

NEILSON VOYNE SMITH

The penguins that spent most
of their time fighting were
the ones with no chicks.

MARIA SEMPLE

I was a round little man
with a heavy heart but a
hopeful spirit. I didn't really
run, or even jog. I waddled.
I was a Penguin. This was
the image that fit.

JOHN BINGHAM

Modern war is distinguished by the fact that all the participants are ostensibly unwilling. We are swept towards one another like colonies of heavily armed penguins on an ice floe.

NICK HARKAWAY

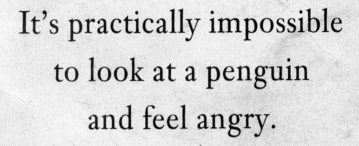

It's practically impossible
to look at a penguin
and feel angry.

JOE MOORE

I can't imagine a single
scenario where I'd have to kill
a penguin to survive.

BENEDICT CUMBERBATCH

All penguins are the same below the surface, which I think is as perfect an analogy as we're likely to get for the futility of racism.

RUSSELL BRAND

3 out of 4 voices in my head
want to sleep; the other wants to
know if penguins have knees.

INTERNET MEME REFERENCING
DAVID FELDMAN

[Penguins] spend their whole lives yelling at the world and each other. They yell at their loved ones, they yell at their enemies, they yell at their dinner, they yell at the big bustling world.

DIANE ACKERMAN

... eyes cold enough to make a penguin wish it had stocked up on thermal underwear.

IAN BARKER

I drove out to the zoo, used the
public facilities, and looked at
penguins. Most people like them,
but I feel sorry for them, trapped
in their formal wear with nowhere
to go and no understanding of
what life is all about once they've
been removed from their habitat —
like a lot of people …

L.E. MODESITT JR

You can't release penguins on their own … they simply won't go without a fellow creature of their own kind.

TOM MICHELL

Watching the destruction of our planet makes me feel as gloomy as a penguin in a pigpen.

D.J. MILNE

Batman never had to get together a petition with 250,000 signatures on it when he wanted to change things. He just went and rammed the Batcar into the Penguin's den.

CAITLIN MORAN

If you march your Winter Journeys you will have your reward, so long as all you want is a penguin's egg.

APSLEY CHERRY-GARRARD

I'm the luckiest penguin
in the world.

ROBIN LORD TAYLOR

The penguin wasn't lost.
He was just lonely.

OLIVER JEFFERS

Don't believe what you hear about those penguins. A species of lazy waddlers. Their extinction is imminent.

BENSON BRUNO

In other words, I was a
moderately happy penguin
who was occasionally
attacked by sadness.

TAKUJI ICHIKAWA

The answer to every problem
involved penguins.

RICK RIORDAN

When you think about things,
think about a can opener
for penguins.

ANTHONY T. HINCKS

Also by Exisle Publishing ...

WOOF

A book of happiness for dog lovers

ANOUSKA JONES

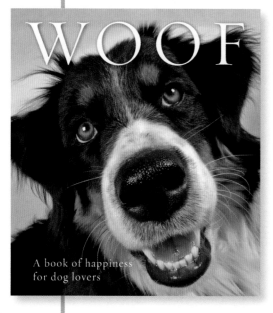

Dogs make our lives feel complete. They're there for us through good times and bad, with their wholehearted engagement in life a lesson to us all on 'living in the moment'.

This is the perfect gift for any dog lover, with its selection of quotes ranging from the serious to the light-hearted, accompanied by beautiful photography.

ISBN 978 1 925335 57 6 (paperback)
ISBN 978 1 925335 09 5 (hardback)

SPIRIT

A book of happiness for horse lovers

ANOUSKA JONES

Horses are the epitome of grace, power and freedom. They also have an ability to touch our souls and connect with our hearts in a way that few other animals can. From a little girl's first pony to a gnarled cowboy's last quarter horse, they can offer us some of our deepest friendships and inspire us to be the best version of ourselves.

Spirit: A book of happiness for horse lovers is a compendium of enduring quotes that capture the essence of our affection for these magnificent animals. Some are by famous people (Winston Churchill, Nathaniel Hawthorne, William Faulkner, Dale Carnegie, William Shakespeare, Ralph Waldo Emerson), others not; some are philosophical, others light-hearted — all are memorable. Accompanied by beautiful photography, and presented in a high-quality gift format, this is a collection of quotes to treasure.

ISBN 978 1 925335 51 4

First published 2019

Exisle Publishing Pty Ltd
PO Box 864, Chatswood, NSW 2057, Australia
226 High Street, Dunedin, 9016, New Zealand
www.exislepublishing.com

A CiP record for this book is available from the National Library of Australia.

ISBN 978 1 925335 91 0

Designed by Big Cat Design
Typeset in Archetype 24 on 36pt
Printed in China

This book uses paper sourced under ISO 14001 guidelines from well-managed forests
and other controlled sources.

2 4 6 8 10 9 7 5 3 1

Photographic credits
Adeliepenguin: page 108; Andreanita: cover spine; Rinus Baak: pages 62, 130; Andrea Basile: pages 8, 18, 42, 132, 156; Rafael Ben Ari: page 64; Henk Bentlage: page 40; Musat Christian: page 24; Gentoo Multimedia: front cover, page 54; goinyk: pages 14, 48, 72, 138; Ben Goode: back cover (bottom & 2nd from right), pages 2–3, 82, 88, 128; Stefano Heusch: page 22; Kmiragaya: page 140; Dalia Kvedaraite: back cover (far left & far right), pages 32, 56; Richard Lindie: pages 70, 92, 152; Mzphoto11: page 60; nastenkin: page 110; Ng Zheng Hui: page 136; Nosnibor137: pages 44, 142; Etienne Oosthuizen: page 66; pilipenkoD: page 118; Vladimir Seliverstov: pages 106, 112; Luc Sesselle: page 80; slew11: pages 4, 12; Stockfreeimages.com: pages 126, 148; Stock.xchng: page 102; Thethirdman: page 16; Yelka: page 84.

Lloyd Spencer Davis
Professor Lloyd Spencer Davis (aka Professor Penguin)
has been studying penguins for over 40 years. He has
written seven books about penguins and published many
scientific articles about them.